Quick and Easy Grilling Recipes

Grilling Made Easy

Justin A. Bryant

ISBN-13: 978-1484160251

CONTENTS

GENERAL GRILLING TIPS 7

CHICKEN 9

CHICKEN GRILLING TIPS 9

    HAWAIIAN CHICKEN TERIYAKI 10
    LIMEY CHICKEN 11
    SUNNY DAY CHICKEN 12
    CHIPOTLE CHICKEN 13
    BROILED BUTTERMILK CHICKEN 14
    BBQ CHICKEN 15
    BEER BUTT CHICKEN 16
    HONEY-LEMON CHICKEN 18
    CHICKEN FAJITAS 19
    GRILLED CHICKEN BREAST 20
    RANCH GRILLED CHICKEN 21
    HONEY MUSTARD GRILLED CHICKEN 22
    CHINESE BARBECUED CHICKEN 23
    MARINATED CHICKEN BREASTS 24
    GRILLED SALSA CHICKEN 25
    AUSSIE BBQ CHICKEN 26

FISH 28

FISH GRILLING TIPS 28

    DELICIOUS ORANGE ROUGHY 29
    EASY GRILLED TILAPIA 30
    GRILLED FILLETS OF COD 31
    JALAPENO TUNA STEAKS 32
    MARINATED SHRIMP 33
    SALMON WITH DILL SAUCE 34
    GLAZED SALMON 36
    SIZZLING SALMON STEAKS 37
    GRILLED SALMON 38
    GRILLED GARLIC SHRIMP 39
    LEMON-GINGER SALMON 40

BEEF 42

BEEF GRILLING TIPS..42

GRILLED HAMBURGER TIP 42

HAMBURGERS 43

EASY GRILLED HAMBURGERS 43
BEST HAMBURGERS 44
CAESAR BURGERS 45

STEAK 46

LONDON BROIL 47
BEEF KABOBS..48
CHUCK WAGON STEAK 50
JAPANESE STEAKS 51
TERIYAKI FINGER STEAKS...52
MARINATED GRILLED STEAK 53
CHUCK ROAST ON GRILL 54
MARINATED BEEF TENDERLOIN 55
BARBECUE BEEF RIBS 56

PORK 58

PORK GRILLING TIPS 58

RIBS..59

BASIC RIBS 59
BARBECUED SPARE RIBS...60
ASIAN RIBS..61
BEST BBQ RIBS 62
FAST BARBECUED SPARERIBS 63
COUNTRY-STYLE PORK RIBS..64

OTHER PORK..65

PORK FRUIT KABOBS 65
GRILLED PORK CHOPS 66
SOUTHWESTERN KABOBS 67
CORIANDER PEPPER PORK 68
PORK TENDERLOIN WITH MUSTARD 69

MARINATED PORK ROAST 70
HONEY GRILLED TENDERLOINS 72

HOT DOGS 75
HOT DOG AND SAUSAGE GRILLING TIPS...75
BACON HOT DOG 76
MESSY HOT DOG 77
CHEESE CHILI DOG 78
BEAN DOGS..79
DOG KABOBS...80
HOT DOG ROLLS 81

TURKEY..83
TURKEY GRILLING TIPS...83
GRILLED TURKEY..84
TURKEYAK 85
CHILI TURKEY BURGERS 86
TURKEY BURGERS 87
TERIYAKI TURKEY STEAKS 88

VEGETABLES 90
VEGETABLE GRILLING TIPS 90
BAKED ONIONS 91
COLDWATER CANYON CORN 92
GRILLED ZUCCHINI SPEARS 93
GREAT GRILLED VEGGIES...94
BUTTERY GARLIC MUSHROOMS...95

MARINADES 97
FLANK STEAK MARINADE 97
ISLAND STEAK MARINADE 98
SOY STEAK MARINADE 99
STEAK MARINADE...100

MEAT OR FOWL MARINADE 101

BEEFY MARINADE 102

CHILI SAUCE MARINADE 103

ONE-FOR-ALL MARINADE (BEEF, PORK, CHICKEN) 104

SAUCES 106

MOLASSES GLAZE FOR RIBS 106

PINEAPPLE SALSA 107

TERIYAKI GLAZE FOR RIBS 108

BBQ SAUCE 109

HOT SAUCE 110

TOMATO BARBECUE SAUCE 111

SPICY BARBECUE SAUCE 112

BARBECUE BASTE FOR CHICKEN (OR PORK CHOPS) 113

STEAK TERIYAKI SAUCE 114

BARBEQUE SAUCE FOR CHICKEN 115

DIFFERENT BARBECUE SAUCE 116

SIDE DISHES 118

GARBAGE BREAD 118

POTATOES ON THE GRILL 119

BBQ-SIDE GARDEN SALAD 120

General Grilling Tips

Keep your grill clean. If you scrub the rack with a grate cleaner or wire brush while it's still warm, it cleans up quickly and is ready for your next grilling extravaganza.

Keep a spray bottle filled with water handy. This is indispensable for killing flare-ups and a spritz or two is a refreshing way to keep the cook cool as well.

Don't crowd your food on the grill. Give everything a little breathing room. Food will cook more evenly with no invasion of its personal space.

Direct grilling means you put the food directly over the heat source. Most typical meat cuts are prepared with this method.

Indirect grilling means you off-set the food from the heat source for heat without the direct intensity. This is great for food that requires a long cooking time. Whole chickens, turkeys and roasts should be prepared with indirect grilling to ensure the entire piece is cooked properly.

Always use tongs or a spatula to turn your food on the grill. Piercing the flesh with a knife or fork allows juices to escape and will result in a dry cut of meat.

Oil your rack to aid in preventing food from sticking to the grill.

Grilling baskets are great for small or narrow pieces of food. These baskets should also be sprayed with oil to prevent sticking.

Chicken
recipes

Chicken

Chicken Grilling Tips

Chicken cooks quickly, so don't leave your grill unattended. No quick trips to the cooler for refreshments or wandering away to check out the ball scores.

If you're planning on grilling a whole chicken, pour a little beer in the main body cavity. This keeps the meat moist and creates a steaming action that helps to cook the meat thoroughly.

Even if you don't plan on eating it, leave the skin on your chicken. It holds in moisture, and you can use it to insert seasonings. Just make a little pocket between the skin and meat and insert your spices into it. Add a little butter to increase flavor and moisture.

Blend seasonings with oil before rubbing on your chicken. The oil holds in moisture and intensifies the flavor of your seasonings.

If you're using a sweet basting sauce, wait until the last 5-10 minutes before applying the coating. Sugar can quickly caramelize and burn, so save it for the end of your grilling process.

Marinate chicken at least 30 minutes to give the mixture ample time to permeate the meat.

Hawaiian Chicken Teriyaki

INGREDIENTS:

12 boneless, skinless chicken breasts

3/4 cup brown sugar

3/4 cup low sodium soy sauce

1 clove fresh garlic, chopped

Small chunk (3/4") crushed fresh ginger

1 tablespoon sesame oil

2 tablespoons sherry

1/2 bunch green onions, finely chopped

1 tablespoon roasted sesame seeds

INSTRUCTIONS:

Combine all ingredients, except chicken breasts, to make the marinade. Marinate chicken breasts for 2 to 4 hours. Grill chicken until done, about 10 to 12 minutes, turning once halfway through grilling time.

Yield: Serves 12.

 **Limey Chicken**

INGREDIENTS:

4 boneless chicken breasts

1/3 cup olive oil

Juice of 3 limes

4 cloves of garlic, minced

3 tablespoons chopped fresh cilantro

1/2 teaspoons salt

1/2 teaspoons pepper

INSTRUCTIONS:

Place the chicken in a 9x13-inch dish. Combine the olive oil, lime juice, garlic, cilantro, salt and pepper in a bowl and mix well. Pour over the chicken. Refrigerate, covered, for 1 hour. Preheat the grill. Grill the chicken for 10 to 12 minutes.

Yield: Serves 4.

Sunny Day Chicken

INGREDIENTS:

1 frying chicken, cut up

1/4 cup prepared mustard

1/4 cup undiluted lemonade concentrate

1/4 cup honey

INSTRUCTIONS:

Mix mustard, honey and lemonade concentrate. Place chicken on grill. Brush with half of the sauce. Grill for 15 minutes. Turn and brush with remaining sauce. Continue grilling for 20 to 30 minutes or until tender.

Yield: Serves 4 to 6.

 # Chipotle Chicken

INGREDIENTS:

4 boneless chicken breasts

1/2 cup barbecue sauce

3 tablespoons onion, chopped

1 tablespoon chipotle chilies

INSTRUCTIONS:

In a small bowl, mix the barbecue sauce, onion and chilies together. Brush one side of each chicken breast with sauce. Grill chicken, sauce side down, for 5 to 8 minutes. Brush the other side of chicken breast with sauce, turn chicken and grill for an additional 5 to 8 minutes, or until chicken is tender.

Yield: Serves 4.

Broiled Buttermilk Chicken

INGREDIENTS:

2 cups buttermilk

2 tablespoons lemon juice

2 teaspoons salt

1 teaspoon Tabasco

1 teaspoon ground coriander

1 teaspoon paprika

1 1/2 lbs. chicken, cut up, with bones

INSTRUCTIONS:

Mix buttermilk, lemon juice and seasonings in a bowl. Place chicken in a shallow dish or large Ziploc bag and pour buttermilk mixture over chicken. Marinate several hours or overnight in the refrigerator. Grill chicken until done, about 35 to 45 minutes, turning once halfway through grilling time.

Yield: Serves 2.

 # BBQ Chicken

INGREDIENTS:

2 lbs. chicken, with bones

1 1/2 quarts water

2 1/2 teaspoons Worcestershire sauce

2 teaspoons garlic salt

1/2 cup sugar

1/2 cup salt

2 teaspoons pepper

1 1/3 cups vinegar

INSTRUCTIONS:

Combine water, Worcestershire sauce, garlic salt, sugar, salt, pepper and vinegar in a deep pan. Heat to boiling. Parboil desired amount of chicken for 20 minutes. Remove chicken and brown on the grill, basting with the sauce, until tender.

Yield: Serves 3.

Beer Butt Chicken

INGREDIENTS:

1 whole chicken, cleaned, skin on

1 can of beer

Mix:

1 teaspoon salt

1 teaspoon garlic salt

1 teaspoon onion salt

1 teaspoon paprika

1 teaspoon brown sugar

1/4 teaspoon cayenne pepper

INSTRUCTIONS:

Trim the excess fat from the chicken. Rinse the chicken inside and out; pat dry. In a small bowl, combine all ingredients in the mix. Rub about 1 teaspoon of the mix on the inside of the chicken. Rub remaining mix over surface of the chicken.

Open beer and pour off about half the beer. Ease the chicken over the beer can, feet down, until chicken is resting on the can and its legs. The beer can must remain upright at all times.

Charcoal Grill - Spread a few smoked hickory chips over hot charcoal that has ashed over. Place the chicken and beer can on the grill. Close lid but leave vents open. Grill for two hours or until chicken's wings and legs wiggle easily. Add 6 to 8 briquettes to the fire every 30 minutes.

Gas Grill - Set chicken and beer can on aluminum pan to catch drippings. Grill on low for about 1 hour (use meat thermometer to test for doneness, until it registers 180 degrees). Spray chicken while cooking with apple juice mixed with a little vinegar.

Honey-Lemon Chicken

INGREDIENTS:

3 lbs. chicken parts

1/4 cup honey

2 tablespoons lemon juice

1 tablespoon prepared mustard

3/4 teaspoon salt

INSTRUCTIONS:

Grill the chicken for 25 minutes until golden. Meanwhile, in a small bowl, mix honey, lemon juice, mustard and salt. When the chicken is golden, brush generously with some of the honey mixture. Turn chicken pieces skin side up; grill for 10 minutes. Brush with the remaining sauce; grill for 10 minutes longer or until the chicken is fork tender.

Yield: Serves 4.

 # Chicken Fajitas

INGREDIENTS:

1 cup picante sauce

1/4 cup vegetable oil

1 teaspoon lemon juice

Dash of pepper

Dash of garlic powder

Large Ziploc bag

1 1/2 lbs. chicken breasts (boneless & skinless)

INSTRUCTIONS:

Combine the first 5 ingredients and place in large Ziploc bag. Add chicken. Marinate in refrigerator at least 3 hours, up to 24 hours, turning several times. Drain the chicken and grill 10 to 12 minutes until thoroughly cooked. Slice meat into thin strips.

Serve with:

Flour tortillas
Chopped tomatoes
Onions
Shredded cheese
Sour cream

 Grilled Chicken Breast

INGREDIENTS:

3/4 cup red wine vinegar

1 1/2 cups chili sauce

2 cloves garlic (halved)

1 1/2 teaspoons prepared horseradish

1 teaspoon salt

4 chicken breasts, with bones

INSTRUCTIONS:

Mix the vinegar, chili sauce, garlic, horseradish and salt in bowl. Set aside half of marinade. Place chicken in shallow dish. Pour marinade over chicken. Turn the chicken so each piece is well coated. Cover and marinate in refrigerator for 15 minutes.

Remove chicken from marinade; discard marinade. Place chicken on grill, turning and basting often with part of the reserved marinade (about 30 to 45 minutes). Heat remaining marinade and serve with chicken.

Yield: Serves 4.

 # Ranch Grilled Chicken

INGREDIENTS:

8 chicken breasts, boneless, skinless

Ranch salad dressing mix

Salt & pepper

INSTRUCTIONS:

Roll damp chicken into Ranch dressing mix until well coated. Sprinkle with salt and pepper. Marinate in refrigerator for at least an hour. Then grill until chicken is done, about 10 to 12 minutes.

Yield: Serves 8.

Honey Mustard Grilled Chicken

INGREDIENTS:

4 boneless chicken breasts

1/2 cup mayonnaise

1 teaspoon honey

2 teaspoons mustard

INSTRUCTIONS:

Mix together mayonnaise, mustard and honey. Place chicken breasts on grill. Brush with 1/2 of the sauce. Grill for 6 minutes. Turn and brush with remaining sauce. Continue grilling for 6 to 10 minutes or until tender.

Yield: Serves 4.

Chinese Barbecued Chicken

INGREDIENTS:

1/4 cup soy sauce

3 tablespoons brown sugar

1 garlic clove, minced

1 tablespoon vegetable oil

1 teaspoon dry mustard

1 1/2 teaspoons ginger

2 lbs. chicken with bones, skin removed

INSTRUCTIONS:

Mix the soy sauce, brown sugar, garlic clove, oil, dry mustard, and ginger in a 2 quart microwave-safe dish. Add chicken and coat with sauce mixture. Let chicken marinate in sauce for at least one hour in refrigerator. Grill chicken until done, about 35 to 45 minutes, turning once halfway through grilling time.

Yield: Serves 3 to 4.

 Marinated Chicken Breasts

INGREDIENTS:

4 boneless chicken breasts

Marinade:

3/4 cup cider vinegar
1/2 cup light brown sugar
6 tablespoons vegetable oil
3 tablespoons Dijon mustard
1 tablespoon lime juice
1 tablespoon lemon juice
1 1/2 teaspoons salt
2 cloves garlic (or 1/4 teaspoon garlic powder)
1/8 teaspoon black pepper
1/4 teaspoon parsley

INSTRUCTIONS:

Mix marinade ingredients together and pour over chicken breasts that have been split and laid in a shallow container. Marinate chicken breasts 8 hours in refrigerator. Grill chicken until done, about 10 to 12 minutes, turning once halfway through grilling time.

Yield: Serves 4.

 # Grilled Salsa Chicken

INGREDIENTS:

1 fryer chicken (about 3 pounds), quartered

Cayenne pepper

Pepper

Salt

1 jar (16 oz.) salsa (hot, medium or mild)

1 can (8 oz.) tomato sauce

4 green onions, coarsely chopped

INSTRUCTIONS:

Arrange chicken pieces in a 9x13-inch baking dish (remove skin to reduce calories). Season with salt, pepper and cayenne pepper to taste. Combine salsa and tomato sauce and pour over chicken. Scatter chopped green onions over top. Cover with foil and bake at 350 degrees for 45 minutes.

Heat barbecue grill. Brush grill with oil to keep chicken from sticking. Remove chicken from oven. Carefully lift chicken pieces from sauce, reserving sauce for later use. Place chicken on hot barbecue and grill for 2 or 3 minutes on each side, or until nicely browned. Serve chicken and sauce with hot tortillas, rice and tossed green salad. Yield: Serves 4.

Aussie BBQ Chicken

INGREDIENTS:

2 to 3 lbs. chicken pieces, with bones

5 ounces butter

1 1/2 teaspoons salt

1/8 teaspoon black pepper

Juice of 2 limes

1/4 cup tomato sauce

3 drops Tabasco sauce

1 teaspoon dried thyme

1 clove garlic, crushed

INSTRUCTIONS:

Wash and dry chicken pieces. Melt butter in saucepan, add remaining ingredients and stir. Brush chicken with butter sauce and grill skin side up over a hot fire for 20 minutes. Turn and cook 20 to 25 minutes other side. Baste occasionally.

Yield: Serves 4.

Fish
recipes

Fish

Fish Grilling Tips

Rub oil on the surface of the fish or your grill before cooking the meat. This flesh and skin sticks very easily, and you'll wind up with toasted fish crumbles if you don't make sure you have a non-stick surface.

Choose fish portions with uniform thickness throughout the piece. If you have a fillet that's thick on one end and thin on the other, cut it into two pieces. Start cooking the thick portions. When they're about halfway done, throw on the thin cuts, so everything will be done at roughly the same time.

Fish is rather fragile, and fillets are the most delicate. Whole fish and steaks are a little less frail and can stand up to a novice griller.

Dots of butter and sprinkles of lemon juice add moisture and flavor to your fish as it is grilling. Be careful of the butter, however, as it burns easily.

If you're cooking a whole fish, try adding fresh herbs and a few slices of lemon inside the body cavity. The herbs add flavor and the lemon increases the moisture content. This also opens the space so heat can pass through and evenly cooks the meat.

Delicious Orange Roughy

INGREDIENTS:

4 fillets of orange roughy

1/2 teaspoon lemon rind, grated

2 tablespoons lemon juice

1/4 teaspoon salt

1/2 teaspoon thyme

1/4 teaspoon paprika

1/8 teaspoon garlic powder

4 lemon slices

INSTRUCTIONS:

In a medium size bowl, mix together lemon rind, lemon juice, salt, thyme, paprika and garlic powder; marinate for thirty minutes in refrigerator. Grill the orange roughy on both sides basting often with marinade. Fish should be flaky when done. Garnish with lemon slices.

Yield: Serves 4.

Easy Grilled Tilapia

INGREDIENTS:

1 fillet of tilapia

1 clove of garlic

1/8 teaspoon salt

1/8 teaspoon black pepper

1 slice of lemon

1 cube of ice

Aluminum foil

INSTRUCTIONS:

Lay out a square of foil, enough to fully cover the fillet. Place the slice of lemon on the foil. Cut the clove of garlic in half and rub on both sides of the tilapia, then place garlic clove on foil. Put the tilapia fillet on top of lemon and garlic on foil, sprinkle with pepper and salt.

Put the ice cube on the fillet and fold foil over fish to make a packet. Place foil packet on a medium heated grill for 10 to 15 minutes. Be careful when opening packet once fish is done.

Yield: Serves 1.

Grilled Fillets of Cod

INGREDIENTS:

4 cod fillets, 2 lbs.

1/8 teaspoon salt

1/8 teaspoon pepper

1 teaspoon cumin

1 teaspoon cayenne pepper (optional)

2 tablespoons brown mustard, spicy

1 tablespoon butter, melted

1 lemon

INSTRUCTIONS:

Sprinkle fillets with salt, pepper, cumin and cayenne. Spread brown mustard over fillets. Place fillets on grill and cook 3 to 4 minutes on each side, basting with melted butter. Fish should flake easily with a fork when done. Serve fish with a wedge of lemon.

Yield: Serves 4.

Jalapeno Tuna Steaks

INGREDIENTS:

1 lb. tuna steaks

3 garlic cloves

1 jalapeno pepper

2 1/2 teaspoons lime juice

1 tablespoon olive oil

Salt and pepper to taste

INSTRUCTIONS:

Chop the garlic cloves and jalapeno pepper into very small pieces. In a bowl, whisk together the garlic, jalapeno pepper, lime juice, oil, salt and pepper. Place the steaks on a shallow dish. Pour marinade over steaks and marinate in refrigerator for 30 minutes.

Preheat grill on high heat and oil the grate lightly. Cook steaks for 5 to 7 minutes on each side. Steaks should be firm and hot in the middle when done.

Marinated Shrimp

INGREDIENTS:

1/3 cup olive oil

1/3 cup soy sauce

1/2 teaspoon sugar

1/4 teaspoon garlic powder

1/4 teaspoon ground ginger

2 lbs. large fresh shrimp, peeled & deveined

INSTRUCTIONS:

Mix the olive oil, soy sauce, sugar, garlic powder and ginger in a shallow dish. Reserve 1/4 cup of marinade. Add shrimp, gently tossing to coat. Cover and refrigerate for 2 to 3 hours, stirring occasionally. Drain the marinade and dispose of. Place shrimp on 6 skewers. Grill over medium hot coals for 5 to 6 minutes on each side, frequently basting with reserved marinade.

Yield: Serves 4 to 6.

Salmon with Dill Sauce

INGREDIENTS:

1 1/2 lb. salmon fillet

1 tablespoon olive oil

1/2 teaspoon dried dill

1/4 teaspoon pepper

Dill Sauce:

1 cup chicken broth

1 tablespoon spicy brown mustard

1 tablespoon cornstarch

3/4 cup evaporated milk

2 teaspoons lemon juice

1/2 cup chopped fresh dill

Heavy duty aluminum foil

INSTRUCTIONS:

Preheat grill. Cut salmon fillet into 4 to 6 pieces. Place salmon on a large piece of foil. Brush both sides with olive oil. Sprinkle with pepper and dried dill. Fold foil over top and seal the ends. Grill salmon 4 inches from medium heat for 20 minutes or until fish flakes easily with a fork. Be careful not to overcook.

Dill Sauce - Combine broth, mustard, cornstarch and milk in a bowl. Add lemon juice and fresh dill and mix well. Cook in a small saucepan, stirring constantly, over medium heat until thickened. Place salmon on serving plate and pour sauce on top.

Yield: Serves 4 to 6.

Glazed Salmon

INGREDIENTS:

4 teaspoons spicy brown mustard

3 teaspoons dark brown sugar

1 teaspoon soy sauce

1 teaspoon vinegar

2 salmon fillets

INSTRUCTIONS:

Preheat grill at medium high heat. Mix brown sugar, mustard and soy sauce in a medium bowl with a whisk. Put one tablespoon of the mustard mixture in a small bowl; whisk in vinegar and set aside for serving. Brush one side of salmon with half of the glaze from the medium bowl.

Place salmon glazed side down onto grill. Grill until glaze is barely charred, about 4 minutes. Brush the top portion of the salmon with the remaining glaze from the medium bowl. Turn the salmon over and grill until the second side is slightly charred, approximately 5 minutes. To serve, drizzle reserved glaze from small bowl over salmon.

Yield: Serves 2.

Sizzling Salmon Steaks

INGREDIENTS:

1/4 cup balsamic vinegar

1/4 cup chili sauce

1/4 cup light brown sugar, packed

1 garlic clove, minced

1 tablespoon fresh parsley, chopped

1 teaspoon fresh ginger, grated

1/2 teaspoon cayenne pepper

1/2 teaspoon crushed red pepper flakes

2 (6-ounce) salmon steaks or fillets

INSTRUCTIONS:

Combine the balsamic vinegar, chili sauce, brown sugar, garlic, parsley, ginger, cayenne pepper and red pepper flakes in a medium bowl and mix well. Reserve 1/8 cup of the marinade. Place the salmon steaks in the rest of the marinade and marinate, covered, in the refrigerator for 1 hour.

Remove the salmon steaks from the marinade, disposing of marinade. Grill over hot coals on an oiled grill rack for 4 to 5 minutes per side or until fish flakes, basting occasionally with the reserved marinade. Yield: Serves 2.

Grilled Salmon

INGREDIENTS:

3/4 teaspoon dill weed

1/2 teaspoon lemon pepper seasoning

1/2 teaspoon salt

1/4 teaspoon garlic powder

1 1/2 lbs. salmon

3 teaspoons soy sauce

1/4 cup packed brown sugar

3 teaspoons vegetable oil

3 teaspoons chicken broth

3 teaspoons green onions, chopped

INSTRUCTIONS:

Place salmon in a shallow pan. Sprinkle dill, lemon pepper, salt, and garlic powder on salmon. Combine soy sauce, brown sugar, oil, chicken broth and green onions. Pour on top of salmon. Cover and refrigerate 1 hour, turning at least once. Drain and discard marinade. Grill over hot coals on an oiled grill rack for 4 to 5 minutes per side or until fish flakes.

Yield: Serves 4.

Grilled Garlic Shrimp

INGREDIENTS:

1 1/2 cups table salt (to brine shrimp in)

2 lbs. large raw shrimp in the shell

1 large clove of garlic

1 teaspoon salt

2 teaspoons olive oil

2 teaspoons lemon juice

2 teaspoons fresh oregano leaves, chopped

Lemon wedges

INSTRUCTIONS:

Pour 2 cups hot water into a gallon-sized Ziploc bag. Add the salt, stirring to dissolve; cool to room temperature. Add 3 cups ice water along with the shrimp and let stand 20 to 25 minutes. Drain and rinse thoroughly under cold water.

Mince the garlic clove; sprinkle the salt over it and drag the side of a knife over and over it pressing down until it forms a paste. Add the olive oil, lemon juice and oregano. Toss the brined and rinsed shrimp with the garlic mixture. Place on skewers or in a grill basket and grill 5 to 6 minutes until pink, turning once during cooking.

Yield: Serves 4 to 6.

Lemon-Ginger Salmon

INGREDIENTS:

2 tablespoons teriyaki sauce

2 teaspoons lemon juice

1 small piece ginger root, grated (about 3")

2 (5 ounce) salmon fillets or steaks

2 green onions, sliced

Lemon wedges, for garnish

INSTRUCTIONS:

Combine teriyaki sauce, lemon juice, grated ginger root and green onions. Pour over salmon and marinate at least 1 hour in refrigerator. Grill salmon over hot coals, turning once. Cook 6 to 8 minutes per side, or until fish flakes when tested with fork. Garnish with lemons and serve.

Yield: Serves 2.

Beef
recipes

Beef

Beef Grilling Tips

Choose the right cut of meat. Fat marbling keeps the meat moist. Very lean cuts dry out quickly, so look for a cut with some clean, white fat speckled throughout the meat. Thin cuts of beef cook very quickly, so be careful not to overcook it.

Season your steaks 15 minutes before grilling. This gives the salt and flavors time to melt and seep into the tissue.

Allow meat to come to room temperature before grilling. It absorbs the seasoning more readily and cooks more quickly.

Allow the grill to heat up to the proper temperature before putting the steak on to cook. You want the meat to sear quickly to hold in the juices and maintain its moist texture.

Grilled Hamburger Tip

After you make the hamburger patties, depress the center of the pattie so that the edges are thicker than the middle. It will look like a shallow bowl. Season and place on the grill. Doing this will make the burgers cook evenly and they will retain their juices. Don't flatten while cooking and only turn the hamburgers once.

Hamburgers

 # Easy Grilled Hamburgers

INGREDIENTS:

2 lbs. hamburger

1 egg, beaten

3/4 cup dried bread crumbs or crackers, crushed

1 package ranch dressing mix

1 onion, chopped

Hamburger buns

INSTRUCTIONS:

Mix the egg, bread crumbs, ranch mix and onion together. Add the hamburger and mix well. Make into patties and cook on a hot grill 5 or 6 minutes on one side, flip and grill about 3 to 4 minutes, depending on the grill.

Yield: Serves 6.

 # Best Hamburgers

INGREDIENTS:

3 lbs. ground beef

2 eggs

1 teaspoon Worcestershire sauce

1 envelope Lipton onion soup mix

3 teaspoons steak sauce

Salt and pepper to taste

INSTRUCTIONS:

Mix all ingredients in a large bowl. Form mixture into patties and cook on a hot grill 5 or 6 minutes on one side, flip and grill about 3 to 4 minutes, depending on the grill.

Yield: Serves 8.

 # Caesar Burgers

INGREDIENTS:

1 lb. ground beef

3 tablespoons Parmesan cheese, grated

2 cloves garlic, minced

4 slices mozzarella cheese

Caesar:
2 cups romaine lettuce, torn
2 tablespoons Caesar dressing
1 tablespoon Parmesan cheese, grated

For Buns:
4 tablespoons Caesar dressing

INSTRUCTIONS:

Preheat grill to medium heat. Mix beef, 3 tablespoons of the cheese and the garlic. Form into 4 patties. Grill for 6 minutes on each side, or until meat is cooked. Top with cheese slices. Grill for one minute longer to melt cheese.

Add 2 tablespoons of dressing and 1 tablespoon cheese to the romaine lettuce. Divide the lettuce mixture evenly on bottom halves of buns; add burgers on top and remaining 4 tablespoons dressing. Cover with tops of buns. Yield: Serves 4.

Steak

How long to cook steak:

Thickness	Rare	Medium	Well done
1 inch	3 minutes	5 minutes	6 minutes
1 1/2 inches	4-5 minutes	6-7 minutes	8-9 minutes
2 inches	6-7 minutes	8-9 minutes	9-10 minutes
Internal temperature	140 degrees F	160 degrees F	170 degrees F

 # London Broil

INGREDIENTS:

2 to 3 pounds London broil (or other lean steak)

Marinade:

1/4 cup lemon juice

1/4 cup oil (use beef bouillon for low-fat)

2 teaspoons meat tenderizer

1/4 teaspoons oregano

1 teaspoon Lawry's salt

1/2 teaspoons garlic salt

INSTRUCTIONS:

Mix marinade ingredients together and marinate steak 3 to 8 hours in the refrigerator (pierce and turn occasionally). Grill 10 to 13 minutes or until meat is thoroughly cooked.

Yield: Serves 4.

 # Beef Kabobs

INGREDIENTS:

Sauce:

1/2 cup butter

1/4 cup lemon juice

1 teaspoon prepared mustard

1/8 teaspoon pepper

1 tablespoon Worcestershire sauce

1/2 teaspoon salt

3 teaspoons chives or onions

Kabobs:

2 lbs. sirloin tip, cut into 1-1/2 in. cubes

Green pepper chunks, cut into 1-1/2 in. squares

Cherry tomatoes

Onion, cut into chunks

INSTRUCTIONS:

Sauce - Heat 1/2 cup butter in a small saucepan until it is hot and bubbly. Add lemon juice, mustard, pepper, Worcestershire sauce, salt and onions. Blend and simmer 5 minutes.

Kabobs – Reserve 1/4 cup of sauce. Marinate the meat in remaining sauce for one hour in refrigerator. After placing meat on skewers with vegetables, place on grill 5 or 6 inches from coals and brown slowly 10 or 12 minutes. Turn and brush with sauce. Wrap in foil with sauce inside. Grill on medium coals 10 or 15 minutes.

Yield: 5 kabobs.

 # Chuck Wagon Steak

INGREDIENTS:

3 lbs. roast or round steak

Marinade:

2 tablespoons meat tenderizer

2 tablespoons instant onion

2 teaspoons thyme

1 teaspoon marjoram

1 bay leaf (crushed)

1/2 cup salad oil

1 cup wine vinegar

3 tablespoons lemon juice

1/8 teaspoon pepper

INSTRUCTIONS:

Mix all above ingredients and pour over meat; refrigerate overnight. Dispose of marinade and cook meat on grill, about 1/2 hour on each side.

Yield: Serves 5 to 6.

 # Japanese Steaks

INGREDIENTS:

4 rib-eye steaks

Mix together and place in shallow baking dish or large Ziploc bag:

1/2 cup shoyu sauce (can substitute soy sauce)

1/3 cup sugar

3 crushed garlic

2 pieces crushed ginger

INSTRUCTIONS:

Place raw steaks in dish or bag with marinade and marinate for 2 hours in refrigerator; turn occasionally. Place steaks on barbecue grill and cook until done; for 1" steak, 3 minutes would be rare, 5 minutes for medium and 6 minutes for well done. Adjust as needed.

Yield: Serves 4.

Teriyaki Finger Steaks

INGREDIENTS:

2 lbs. sirloin steak

1/2 cup soy sauce

1/4 cup cider vinegar

1 teaspoon garlic powder

2 teaspoons brown sugar

2 teaspoons onion, chopped

1 teaspoon oil

1/2 teaspoons ground ginger

1/8 teaspoon pepper

INSTRUCTIONS:

lice steak into 1/2-inch strips, place in a large Ziploc bag. Mix together all remaining ingredients; pour over meat in bag. Push the air out of the bag, seal and marinate in refrigerator 2 to 12 hours.

Drain and discard the marinade. Meat can be grilled with or without skewers for 7 to 10 minutes or until meat is thoroughly cooked.

Yield: Serves 4.

# Marinated Grilled Steak

INGREDIENTS:

1 1/2 lbs. trimmed steak, flank or sirloin

1/2 cup soy sauce

1/4 cup dry red wine

Juice from 1 lemon

1 large clove garlic, sliced or minced

3 tablespoons vegetable oil

2 tablespoons Worcestershire sauce

1/8 teaspoon pepper

2 teaspoons dill weed, chopped

6 green onions, chopped

INSTRUCTIONS:

Mix all ingredients, except the steak. Marinate steak in the mixture, turning occasionally, for 6 to 12 hours in refrigerator. Remove from marinade, disposing of marinade.

Cook meat over hot coals until steak is thoroughly cooked - about 5 minutes on each side for rare. Adjust as needed. Slice meat on the diagonal across the grain and serve.

Yield: Serves 4.

 # Chuck Roast on Grill

INGREDIENTS:

3 to 3-1/2 lb. chuck roast - cut rather thick

Adolph's meat tenderizer

4 teaspoons corn oil or canola oil

2 teaspoons Kitchen Bouquet

1 sliced onion (if desired)

INSTRUCTIONS:

Trim fat from meat. Salt well with tenderizer on both sides. With a fork, prick meat to work in tenderizer. Let meat stand for 1 hour in refrigerator. Mix oil and Kitchen Bouquet together and brush mixture over all parts of the meat. Let stand 1 more hour in refrigerator.

Brown roast over charcoal fire or on grill. Place sliced onions on meat. Wrap meat in double heavy duty foil, and place on grill to cook. Roast until

meat is thoroughly cooked. Time will vary because of thickness of meat and temperature of fire, about 1/2 hour on each side.

Yield: 5 to 6 servings.

Marinated Beef Tenderloin

INGREDIENTS:

1 cup red wine

1 small onion, chopped

1 bay leaf

1/2 teaspoon salt

1 tablespoon parsley

1/4 teaspoon thyme

1 clove garlic, crushed

2 lbs. tenderloin steak (1 1/2 inch thick)

INSTRUCTIONS:

Combine wine, onion, bay leaf, salt, parsley, thyme and garlic, mixing well. Pour into a large, shallow dish. Add the steak, cover and marinate in the refrigerator overnight, turning the steak occasionally. Remove steak, discarding marinade and grill 8 or 9 minutes on each side.

Yield: Serves 6.

Barbecue Beef Ribs

INGREDIENTS:

1 rack of beef ribs

3 stalks of celery

2 carrots

1 medium onion

3 beef bouillon cubes

Salt and pepper to taste

Bottle of barbecue sauce

INSTRUCTIONS:

Cut ribs apart and place into a large kettle. Chop vegetables and put on top of ribs. Cover with water and add bouillon cubes, salt, and pepper. Boil until meat is tender. Remove ribs and coat heavily with sauce. Refrigerate at least 2 hours, but best if left overnight. Barbecue on grill until browned and heated through.

Yield: Serves 3 to 4.

Pork recipes

Pork

Pork Grilling Tips

Remember, pork is the other white meat. Most pork is very lean and will dry quickly on the grill. Rub lean cuts with oil or marinade to maintain moisture.

Pork should be cooked on a medium heat approximately 3 to 6 inches from the heat source.

Pork chops and steaks should be at least 3/4 to 1 inch thick so they don't cook too quickly and dry out.

Preheat your grill before cooking pork. This ensures that the heat sears the surface and seals in the juices.

If you're cooking a thick cut like a loin or roast, you'll need two heat zones on your grill. Use the high heat zone to sear all sides of the cut. Then, move it to a lower heat zone to complete cooking the interior of the meat. Make sure to turn the meat often for even cooking.

Have your butcher cut pockets into extra-thick pork chops. Fill the pocket with your favorite stuffing and grill. The bread and vegetable mixture helps to maintain moisture, and you've added a side dish with no extra cooking!

Ribs

 **Basic Ribs**

INGREDIENTS:

6 lbs. country-style pork ribs or 8 pounds spare ribs

1 lemon, sliced

1 onion, sliced

Salt and pepper to taste

2 cups barbecue sauce

INSTRUCTIONS:

Preheat the oven to 325 degrees F. In a large roasting pan, place the ribs on a rack in a single layer. Place the sliced lemon and onion on top and sprinkle with salt and pepper. Add 1/4 inch water, cover, and bake at 325 degrees F for 1 hour.

Remove the ribs from the pan and discard the water, lemon, and onion. Place the ribs on a charcoal grill. Brush 1 cup of the barbecue sauce on top and grill for 15 minutes. Turn the meat over and brush with the remaining sauce. Grill for 10 minutes more.

Yield: Serves 6.

 # Barbecued Spare Ribs

INGREDIENTS:

3 to 5 lbs. spare ribs or western ribs

2 medium onions, sliced

1 cup water

1/2 teaspoon black pepper

1/2 teaspoon red pepper

2 tablespoons vinegar

1 cup ketchup

1 teaspoon chili powder

1 teaspoon paprika

1 tablespoon salt

1/2 cup red wine (optional)

INSTRUCTIONS:

Wash ribs, cut into pieces. Place in pan with sliced onion. Mix the water, black and red pepper, vinegar, ketchup, chili powder, paprika, salt and wine in a bowl and pour sauce over ribs. Cook 2 hours over medium heat on barbecue grill.

Yield: Serves 4.

Asian Ribs

INGREDIENTS:

6 rack of ribs, cut in serving size

2 tablespoons fresh ginger, minced

1 tablespoon garlic, minced

1 1/2 cups ketchup

1 1/2 cups soy sauce

1/2 cup honey

1/3 cup dry sherry

1 tablespoon rosemary, chopped

2 tablespoons scallions, chopped

INSTRUCTIONS:

Parboil ribs for 1 1/2 to 2 hours; cool slightly. Combine ginger, garlic, ketchup, soy sauce, honey, sherry and rosemary. Marinate cooked ribs in the mix overnight or for at least 8 hours in the refrigerator. Cook for 15 minutes on the grill or until ribs are thoroughly cooked. Sprinkle with chopped scallions before serving.

Yield: Serves 12 to 15.

 # Best BBQ Ribs

INGREDIENTS:

2 pounds pork spareribs

1/2 teaspoon salt

Cut pork spareribs into 2 large pieces. Place ribs in a pot, cover ribs with water and add salt. Simmer on stove until tender, about 45 to 60 minutes. Drain.

Sauce:

1/4 cup ketchup
2 tablespoons chili sauce
1 tablespoon brown sugar
1 tablespoon butter
1 tablespoon onion, chopped
2 teaspoons prepared mustard
1 teaspoon Worcestershire sauce
1/8 teaspoon garlic salt
2 thin lemon slices

INSTRUCTIONS:

In a bowl, combine all sauce ingredients. Put in saucepan and bring to a boil; remove from heat.

Grill ribs while they are still hot over medium to low coals about 10 to 15 minutes on each side, basting often with the sauce.

Yield: Serves 2.

Fast Barbecued Spareribs

Precook ribs in the microwave and finish up on the grill, saving lots of time without sacrificing that wonderful barbecue flavor.

INGREDIENTS:

4 pounds lean spareribs cut into individual ribs

Barbecue sauce

INSTRUCTIONS:

Place ribs on their side in a large rectangular dish. Cover loosely with waxed paper and cook on high 18 to 20 minutes until fork tender. (Rearrange ribs after cooking first 10 minutes). Drain and transfer to grill. Cook 10 minutes. Brush with sauce and cook 5 more minutes, turning several times.

Yield: Serves 4.

Country-Style Pork Ribs

INGREDIENTS:

5 to 6 pounds country-style pork ribs

1 bottle barbecue sauce

1/4 cup brown sugar

1 to 2 teaspoons horseradish

1 onion, chopped

2 tablespoons butter, melted

INSTRUCTIONS:

Boil ribs for 45 minutes. Combine barbecue sauce, brown sugar, and horseradish. Sauté onion in butter and add to barbecue sauce mixture. Place ribs on a hot grill, brush with sauce, and cook about 7 minutes on each side.

Yield: Serves 4.

Other Pork
Pork Fruit Kabobs

INGREDIENTS:

1 can (8 oz.) pineapple slices

1/3 cup orange marmalade

2 tablespoons soy sauce

1 1/2 pounds boneless pork, cut into 1" cubes

2 medium cooking apples, cored and cut into 6 wedges each

INSTRUCTIONS:

Drain pineapple, reserving 2 tablespoons syrup. Quarter each slice; set aside. In saucepan, combine reserved syrup, marmalade and soy sauce. Heat until marmalade melts.

Thread 6 skewers alternately with pork, pineapple and apples, Grill over medium coals, about 15 minutes, turning and brushing often with marmalade mixture.

Yield: Serves 6.

Grilled Pork Chops

INGREDIENTS:

6 top loin pork chops

1 cup Italian dressing

1 1/2 teaspoons Worcestershire sauce

Large Ziploc bag

INSTRUCTIONS:

In a bowl, mix the Italian dressing and Worcestershire sauce together. Place the pork chops in a large Ziploc bag, pour the sauce mixture over them and marinate in refrigerator overnight. Remove chops and discard marinade. Grill chops for 8 to 15 minutes.

Yield: Serves 4.

 # Southwestern Kabobs

INGREDIENTS:

4 boneless top sirloin pork chops

1/2 large onion

1/2 green pepper

4 teaspoons taco seasoning

INSTRUCTIONS:

Cut the pork chops, onion and green pepper into 1" pieces. Toss pork cubes with taco seasoning. Alternate pork, onions and green peppers on skewers. Grill 8 to 12 minutes or until done.

Yield: Serves 4.

Coriander Pepper Pork

INGREDIENTS:

4 pork chops (1 1/2-inch thick)

2 cloves garlic, crushed

1 teaspoon ground coriander

8 crushed peppercorns

1 teaspoon brown sugar

3 teaspoons soy sauce

INSTRUCTIONS:

Combine garlic, coriander, peppercorns, brown sugar and soy sauce. Put meat in a shallow baking dish or large Ziploc bag. Pour the sauce over meat and marinate for 1 hour in refrigerator. Grill about 10 to 12 minutes per side, brushing occasionally with sauce.

Yield: Serves 4.

Pork Tenderloin with Mustard

INGREDIENTS:

1/2 cup spicy brown mustard

4 large garlic cloves, crushed

2 tablespoons dried thyme

1/4 teaspoon pepper

2 tablespoons balsamic vinegar

1/4 cup dry red wine

2 tablespoons olive oil

2 pounds pork tenderloin

INSTRUCTIONS:

Combine the mustard, garlic, thyme, pepper, vinegar, wine and olive oil in a large bowl. Add the pork, turning to coat well. Marinate, covered, in the refrigerator for 1 to 10 hours, turning occasionally.

Preheat grill. Remove the pork from the marinade; discard marinade. Grill for 13 to 14 minutes or to 160 degrees on a meat thermometer, turning 3 times and brushing with marinade. Watch carefully to make sure the pork does not become dry. Yield: Serves 8.

Marinated Pork Roast

INGREDIENTS:

3 to 4 lb. rolled pork roast

1/2 cup vegetable oil

1 1/2 cups tomato juice

1/2 cup onion, chopped

1/4 cup lemon juice

1/4 cup parsley, snipped

1 garlic clove, minced

1 teaspoon thyme

1 teaspoon marjoram

1 teaspoon salt

1/2 teaspoon pepper

INSTRUCTIONS:

Combine all ingredients except meat. Place pork in a deep bowl; pour marinade mixture over meat. Cover and refrigerate for 6 hours or overnight. Turn meat occasionally and spoon marinade over meat.

Preheat grill. Place roast on grill over foil drip-pan (with coals to the outside). Grill the roast indirectly for 1 to 2 hours over a medium heat. Cook until done. Use a meat thermometer and the meat will be done when the internal temperature is 160 degrees. (Juices will be clear and a nice brown crust will form on the outside). Turn occasionally and baste frequently with marinade.

Yield: Serves 5 to 6.

Honey Grilled Tenderloins

INGREDIENTS:

2 (3 to 4-pound) pork tenderloins

1/3 cup soy sauce

1/2 teaspoon ginger

5 cloves of garlic, halved

2 tablespoons light brown sugar

3 tablespoons honey

2 teaspoons vegetable oil

Nonstick grilling spray

INSTRUCTIONS:

Prepare medium-hot coals (350 to 400 degrees) in a barbecue grill. Trim the fat from the tenderloins and butterfly by making a lengthwise cut in each. Place meat in a shallow container or in a large heavy-duty Ziploc plastic bag.

Mix the soy sauce, ginger and garlic in a bowl; pour over the tenderloins. Cover or seal bag. Refrigerate for 4 hours, turning occasionally. Remove the tenderloins from the marinade; discard the marinade.

Combine the brown sugar, honey and oil in a small saucepan. Cook over low heat until the brown sugar dissolves. Coat a barbecue grill with nonstick grilling spray. Arrange the tenderloins on the grill over the coals and brush with the honey mixture. Grill for 20 minutes or to 160 degrees on a meat thermometer, basting frequently.

Yield: Serves 6 to 8.

Hot Dog
recipes

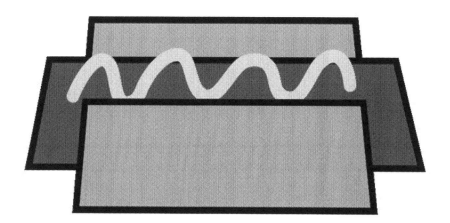

Hot Dogs

Hot Dog And Sausage Grilling Tips

Never, ever use a fork on your sausages. The juices will escape and you'll end up with a dry, tasteless tube of meat. Always use a tong to turn food on a grill. Poking a sausage with a fork can also be dangerous. The super-heated juice and grease can shoot like a geyser from your impromptu poke, and you can end up with a burn, or at least a ruined shirt.

Leave elbow room between hot dogs on a grill. They should be rolled every minute or two so all sides can cook evenly.

You can parboil sausages and just finish them up on the grill. This ensures the meat is cooked all the way through, and then it only takes a few minutes until they're ready to serve.

To reduce the calories of a sausage, you can slice it lengthwise about 80 percent through, and cook it open-face on the grill. Yes, all the juices will run out and they will lose a good deal of flavor and moisture. However, you're also reducing the calories significantly. Anyway, if you add loads of toppings, you won't notice the lack of flavor too much.

Sausages can burn quite easily. Cook them at a lower temperature, and increase the cooking time to create a perfectly grilled sausage sandwich.

Bacon Hot Dog

INGREDIENTS:

1/4 cup onion, chopped

1 fresh jalapeno, chopped

1 tomato, finely chopped

1 package hot dogs

10 slices bacon

10 hot dog buns

1/4 cup mayonnaise

1/4 cup mustard

1/2 cup ketchup

INSTRUCTIONS:

Mix together the onions, jalapenos and tomatoes. Wrap each hot dog with a slice of bacon, tuck to secure. Grill wrapped hot dogs over medium heat for approximately 9 to 12 minutes, turning occasionally. Once the bacon is completely cooked and hot dogs are heated throughout, remove from grill and place on a paper towel. Spread mayonnaise on each side of bun insides and toast the buns on grill, open faced, until light brown and toasted. Place a wrapped hot dog in each bun and top with onion mixture, plus mustard and ketchup.

Yield: Serves 5.

Messy Hot Dog

INGREDIENTS:

16 ounces coleslaw mix

1/4 cup real mayonnaise

1/2 tablespoon spicy brown mustard

1 tablespoon sugar

1 teaspoon honey

1 package hot dog buns

1/2 cup barbecue sauce

8 pickle spears, dill

1 package hot dogs

INSTRUCTIONS:

Preheat the grill. Mix together mayonnaise, coleslaw mix, mustard, sugar and honey. Place hot dogs on the grill and baste them with barbecue sauce. If desired, grill the hot dog buns open faced. Place each grilled hot dogs in a bun and top with barbecue sauce, coleslaw mixture and a pickle spear. Messy and delicious!

Yield: Serves 5.

Cheese Chili Dog

INGREDIENTS:

1 cup corn chips, crushed

8 hot dog buns

8 all-beef hot dogs, bun length

8 ounces pasteurized cheese, cubed

1 can chili without beans, 15 ounces

1 red onion, finely chopped

INSTRUCTIONS:

Cut a split down the center of each hot dog. Grill the hot dogs on a preheated grill, turning occasionally. When the hot dogs are almost done, place cubed cheese into the split in the hot dog and let melt, then remove from the grill.

Toast buns on grill, open faced, until light brown and toasted. Place a hot dog into each toasted bun and top with chili, corn chips and chopped onion.

Yield: Serves 4.

 Bean Dogs

INGREDIENTS:

1 package hot dogs

1 package hot dog buns

Beans as desired

Boston Style:

Split wieners lengthwise, spread with sweet pickle relish, fill with Boston baked beans. Wrap each in double thickness of heavy foil. Grill 5 minutes on coals, turning once. Toast buns on grill.

Southwest Style:

Split wieners lengthwise and fill with chili beans. Wrap each in double thickness of heavy foil. Grill 5 minutes on coals, turning once. Toast buns on grill.

Arizona Style:

Split wieners lengthwise and fill with spicy chili, no beans. Wrap each in double thickness of heavy foil. Grill 5 minutes on coals, turning once. Toast buns on grill.

Yield: Serves 5.

Dog Kabobs

INGREDIENTS:

1 package hot dogs

1 package hot dog buns

Pineapple chunks, 8 ounces, drained

2 red or yellow peppers, cut into large squares

Vegetable oil

INSTRUCTIONS:

Cut each hot dog into 4 pieces. Alternate hot dog pieces on skewer with pineapple chunks and pepper squares. Brush with vegetable oil. Grill over hot coals, turning until browned. Serve on toasted buns.

Yield: Serves 5.

 Hot Dog Rolls

INGREDIENTS:

1 lb. beef hot dogs, cut crosswise into 1/4 inch slices

3/4 lb. sharp Cheddar cheese, cut into 1/2 inch cubes

1/4 cup onion, minced

1/3 cup stuffed olives, chopped

3 hard-boiled eggs, chopped

1/4 cup chili sauce

1/4 cup mayonnaise

12 hot dog buns

INSTRUCTIONS:

Combine the hot dogs, cheese, onion, olives, eggs, chili sauce and mayonnaise. Open the buns; fill each with about 1/3 cup of hot dog mixture. Wrap each bun in heavy-duty aluminum foil, twisting the ends. To cook, place foil packages on grill for 15 to 20 minutes. Unwrap and serve.

Yield: Makes 12 packets.

Turkey
recipes

Turkey

Turkey Grilling Tips

Because turkey legs are very thick at one end and very thin at the other, it's a good idea to microwave or parboil them for faster, more even cooking on the grill.

Rub oil on pieces of turkey before placing on the grill, or oil the grilling rack to ensure the meat does not stick.

Indirect grilling is best for large pieces like bone-in breasts or whole turkeys. This method allows the center of the meat to cook and prevents burning the outer surface.

Grilling a whole turkey takes a lot of time and effort. Use a turkey that is less than 16 pounds to ensure you won't be postponing your turkey dinner to a midnight snack soiree.

Grilled Turkey

Ingredients:

Marinate 1/4 to 1/2 inch thick turkey breast slices or whole turkey drumsticks for at least three hours or overnight in:

1 cup water

1/8 cup salt (or less to taste)

1/2 cup lemon juice

2 dashes tabasco sauce

1 tablespoon garlic juice

Place meat on grill and baste with a mixture of:

2 tablespoons salt

1/2 cup oil

1/2 cup lemon juice

1/4 cup soy sauce

1 tablespoon oregano leaves

Instructions:

Drumsticks take about 45 minutes to grill. Breast slices take much less time depending on the thickness of the meat.

 **Turkeyak**

INGREDIENTS:

4 lbs. boneless turkey breasts or tenderloins

1/2 cup olive oil

1/2 cup white wine

1/2 cup soy sauce

1 clove garlic, minced

3 tablespoons lemon juice

3 tablespoons brown sugar or honey

INSTRUCTIONS:

Cut turkey into 1-1/2" cubes. Combine remaining ingredients in a bowl. Reserve 1/3 cup of mixture and pour remainder of mixture over turkey meat. Marinate at least for 1 hour in refrigerator.

Place turkey cubes on skewers and grill, turning skewers frequently until meat is browned, for about 20 minutes. Brush often with reserved marinade while cooking.

Yield: 8 to 10 servings.

Chili Turkey Burgers

INGREDIENTS:

1 lb. ground turkey

1/2 cup chili sauce

1/4 cup green pepper, diced

1/3 cup red onion, diced

INSTRUCTIONS:

Combine all ingredients, form into patties and grill approximately 4 minutes per side.

Yield: Serves 4.

 # Turkey Burgers

INGREDIENTS:

1/4 cup spicy brown mustard

3 tablespoons honey

1 lb. ground turkey breast

1/4 teaspoon salt

1/4 teaspoon black pepper

4 hamburger buns

Lettuce leaves, tomato and onion slices for garnish

2 teaspoons Canola oil

INSTRUCTIONS:

Preheat the grill. In a small bowl, whisk together mustard and honey until smooth. (If you heat the honey for a few seconds in the microwave, it makes the blending process a little easier.) In a mixing bowl combine ground turkey with 3 tablespoons of the mustard/honey mixture. Add salt and pepper and mix.

Form the mixture into four patties, each one inch thick. Brush both sides of the burgers with canola oil. Grill until cooked through (be sure there are no pink centers), about 8 minutes per side, but grilling time may vary, so watch closely. Brush occasionally with the honey mustard sauce. Yield: Serves 4.

Teriyaki Turkey Steaks

INGREDIENTS:

1 package Honeysuckle turkey steaks

Teriyaki marinade and sauce

INSTRUCTIONS:

Thaw steaks. Brush with marinade while grilling over medium-hot coals. Steaks are done when juices run clear, about 10 minutes. Serve with rice, pineapple, and green beans.

Yield: Serves 4.

Vegetable recipes

Vegetables

Vegetable Grilling Tips

It's far more effective to precook vegetables and just finish them off on the grill. Here's a list of some vegetables, their precooking times and grilling times:

Vegetable	Precook Time	Grilling Time
Asparagus	3-4 minutes	3-5 minutes
Baby Carrots	3-5 minutes	3-5 minutes
New Potatoes	10 minutes or until almost tender	10-12 minutes

Soak vegetables in cold water before grilling to prevent dryness.

After soaking in water, dry the vegetables with a paper towel and coat with oil. This will prevent sticking to the grill.

Use skewers to prevent small chunks of vegetables from rolling around or falling through the rack. Use two skewers so the pieces don't just roll around on the stick.

Soak corn and husks three hours in cold water before grilling.

Baked Onions

INGREDIENTS:

4 onions

4 beef bouillon cubes

4 teaspoons butter

INSTRUCTIONS:

Using an apple corer, make a hole in each onion. Place 1 bouillon cube and 1 teaspoon butter in each onion. Wrap in foil. Grill for 45 minutes.

Yield: Serves 4.

Coldwater Canyon Corn

INGREDIENTS:

8 to 10 ears of corn

1 tablespoon salt

Water

INSTRUCTIONS:

Soak unhusked corn in salted water that covers the corn for 3 to 4 hours. Remove the corn from the water and drain the corn for 30 minutes. Heat a charcoal grill. Place unhusked corn on the grill and roast, turning frequently, for 10 to 15 minutes until the husks are charred. Remove the husks and serve.

Yield: Serves 4 to 5.

# Grilled Zucchini Spears

INGREDIENTS:

3 medium zucchini

1/4 cup olive oil

5 garlic cloves, crushed

INSTRUCTIONS:

Marinate oil and garlic overnight. Quarter unpeeled zucchini lengthwise. Grill and baste with marinade until tender.

Yield: Serves 6.

Great Grilled Veggies

INGREDIENTS:

3 yellow bell peppers

3 red bell peppers

4 zucchini squash

1/4 cup Italian dressing

1/4 cup Parmesan cheese

INSTRUCTIONS:

Cut zucchini into 1/2 inch thick diagonal slices. Cut bell peppers into 1/2 inch strips. Place veggies into a grilling basket. Grill veggies approximately ten minutes turning the basket occasionally. Place grilled veggies on a serving plate or bowl and coat with dressing and cheese.

 # Buttery Garlic Mushrooms

INGREDIENTS:

1 lb. whole Portobello mushrooms

3 garlic cloves, minced

1/3 cup butter, melted

1/4 teaspoon salt

1/4 teaspoon pepper

1 tablespoon chives, chopped

INSTRUCTIONS:

Wash mushrooms and remove the stems. Mix together garlic, butter, pepper and salt in a small bowl. Brush garlic mixture on dried mushrooms. Place mushrooms on preheated medium-heat grill for eight minutes; turn only once. Remove grilled mushrooms to a serving dish and top with chives.

Marinade
recipes

Marinades

# Flank Steak Marinade

INGREDIENTS:

3/4 cup vegetable oil

3 tablespoons brown sugar

1 onion, chopped

1 1/2 teaspoons garlic salt

1 1/2 teaspoons ginger

2 tablespoons vinegar

Flank steak

INSTRUCTIONS:

Score steak on both sides before putting in the marinade. Mix the vegetable oil, sugar, onion, garlic salt, ginger and vinegar; pour over steak. Marinate overnight, turning the steak a few times. Grill to taste.

Island Steak Marinade

INGREDIENTS:

1 cup soy sauce

1/2 cup brown sugar

1/2 cup vinegar

1/2 cup pineapple juice

1 1/2 teaspoons salt

1 teaspoon garlic powder

INSTRUCTIONS:

Mix all ingredients together. Marinate steak in mixture for 2 to 3 hours in refrigerator or overnight before grilling. Grill to taste.

 # Soy Steak Marinade

INGREDIENTS:

1/2 cup soy sauce

3 tablespoons honey

2 tablespoons vinegar

1/4 teaspoon ginger

3/4 cup vegetable oil

1 onion, chopped

1/2 teaspoon garlic powder

Steak

INSTRUCTIONS:

Mix all ingredients except steak in a shallow dish. Add flank steak to marinate and let stand 24 hours in refrigerator, turning steak occasionally. Grill to taste.

Steak Marinade

INGREDIENTS:

1/2 cup vegetable oil

1/2 cup soy sauce

2 teaspoons vinegar

1 teaspoon onion, minced

1/2 teaspoons ginger

1/8 teaspoon garlic powder

2 lb. steak of your choice

INSTRUCTIONS:

Marinate steak in mixture of oil, soy sauce, vinegar, onion, ginger and garlic powder. Refrigerate several hours or overnight. Turn occasionally. Grill to taste.

Yield: Serves 4 to 6.

Meat or Fowl Marinade

INGREDIENTS:

1/2 cup soy sauce

1/2 cup vegetable oil

1/2 cup sherry or sake

1/3 cup lemon or pineapple juice

2 cloves, crushed

2 tablespoons sugar

1 teaspoon ginger

1 teaspoon salt

INSTRUCTIONS:

Combine all the ingredients and mix well. Reserve 1/4 cup marinade for basting. Marinate several hours or overnight in the refrigerator. Grill to taste. Fantastic for venison, large game, geese, and duck.

 # Beefy Marinade

INGREDIENTS:

1 cup ketchup

1/2 cup wine vinegar

1/2 small onion, chopped

2 cloves garlic, chopped

1 teaspoon Worcestershire sauce

1/2 teaspoon seasoned salt

1/2 teaspoon chili powder

1 teaspoon prepared mustard

INSTRUCTIONS:

Mix all ingredients together. Use over steaks, roast, and other meats. Marinate 2 hours or overnight. Grill to taste.

Chili Sauce Marinade

INGREDIENTS:

1 cup Las Palmas red chili sauce

1 clove garlic

1/2 teaspoon oregano

1/4 cup vinegar

1/4 cup oil

INSTRUCTIONS:

Rinse out Las Palmas can with water and add to above. Reserve 1/3 cup marinade and marinate meat in remaining marinade overnight. Baste with reserved marinade as meat cooks on grill.

 # One-For-All Marinade (Beef, Pork, Chicken)

INGREDIENTS:

1 beef flank steak (1 1/2 lbs.) or pork chops or chicken

3/4 cup orange juice

1/4 cup reduced sodium soy sauce

2 teaspoons prepared mustard

2 teaspoons brown sugar

1 teaspoon canola oil

2 garlic cloves, minced

Large Ziploc bag

INSTRUCTIONS:

In a medium bowl, combine the orange juice, soy sauce, mustard, brown sugar, oil and garlic cloves. Put meat of choice in the Ziploc bag and pour the orange juice mixture in the bag, coating the meat well. Seal the Ziploc bag; refrigerate 4 hours or overnight. Coat grill with nonstick spray. Drain the marinade and discard it. Grill meat.

Sauce recipes

Sauces

 # Molasses Glaze for Ribs

INGREDIENTS:

3/4 cup ketchup

3 tablespoons light molasses

1 1/2 tablespoons soy sauce

1 1/2 tablespoons lemon juice

A few splashes of bottled hot pepper sauce

INSTRUCTIONS:

Mix all ingredients together in a small bowl. Brush glaze on ribs during the last 20 minutes of grilling.

Yield: 3/4 cup.

 # Pineapple Salsa

INGREDIENTS:

1 pineapple, peeled, cored and diced

1 bunch cilantro, chopped

1 jalapeno, seeded and chopped

2 oz. red wine vinegar

1/2 teaspoon Worcestershire sauce

Dash of salt

INSTRUCTIONS:

Mix all ingredients. Serve at room temperature on grilled fish or chicken.

Teriyaki Glaze for Ribs

INGREDIENTS:

1/4 cup soy sauce

1/4 cup unsweetened pineapple juice

1/4 cup dry sherry

2 tablespoons brown sugar

1 tablespoon cornstarch

1/2 teaspoon ground ginger

1 clove garlic, minced

INSTRUCTIONS:

In a saucepan, mix soy sauce, pineapple juice, sherry, brown sugar, cornstarch, ginger and garlic. Cook on medium heat and until bubbly and thickened, stirring often. Cook 2 more minutes, stirring constantly. Brush the glaze on ribs during final 10 minutes of grilling.

Yield: 3/4 cup.

 # BBQ Sauce

INGREDIENTS:

3 tablespoons butter

1/3 cup chopped onion

1/3 cup vinegar

1 cup ketchup

1/2 cup water

2 tablespoons brown sugar

2 teaspoons prepared mustard

1 tablespoon Worchester sauce

Salt and pepper to taste

INSTRUCTIONS:

Melt butter and add chopped onion and sauté until soft. Add rest of ingredients. Bring to boil, cover and simmer for 15 minutes. Stir often. Add salt and pepper to taste. This is great for chicken on the grill. Can be refrigerated for several days.

 # Hot Sauce

INGREDIENTS:

1 cup white vinegar

1 cup cooking oil

1/4 cup salt

3 tablespoons cayenne pepper

1 jalapeno pepper, chopped (optional)

INSTRUCTIONS:

Heat on stove until mixture reaches a rolling boil. Remove from heat. Can be stored in refrigerator and used as needed. This is a great hot sauce recipe for chicken, ribs, and more.

Tomato Barbecue Sauce

INGREDIENTS:

1 can (8 oz.) tomato sauce

1/4 cup corn oil

2 tablespoons vinegar

1 tablespoon prepared mustard

2 tablespoons brown sugar

INSTRUCTIONS:

Combine ingredients in saucepan. Heat until hot. Use sauce on meat last 15 to 20 minutes of grilling time.

# Spicy Barbecue Sauce

INGREDIENTS:

1 cup chili sauce

1/2 cup green pepper, chopped

1 tablespoon onion, minced

1/2 teaspoon horseradish

INSTRUCTIONS:

Combine chili sauce, green pepper, minced onion and horseradish and simmer 10 minutes. Brush on meat last 5 minutes of cooking time. Brush again as removed from grill.

Barbecue Baste For Chicken (Or Pork Chops)

INGREDIENTS:

1 chicken or 6 pork chops

3/4 cup vinegar

1/4 cup water

1/2 cup margarine

3 tablespoons sugar

1 tablespoon salt

INSTRUCTIONS:

Mix all ingredients in saucepan and bring to a boil. Brush on chicken pieces or pork chops several times as they cook on the grill.

 # Steak Teriyaki Sauce

INGREDIENTS:

1/2 cup soy sauce

1/2 cup dry sherry

2 tablespoons sugar

1/2 teaspoon ginger

1/4 teaspoon dry mustard

1/8 teaspoon garlic powder

INSTRUCTIONS:

Mix all ingredients together and pour over steak. Marinate steaks 4 to 6 hours, turning occasionally. Grill until desired doneness.

 # Barbeque Sauce for Chicken

INGREDIENTS:

1/2 cup butter

1 teaspoon poultry seasoning

1/4 teaspoon pepper

2 teaspoons Lawry's seasoned salt

1 teaspoon barbecue spice

2 teaspoons garlic powder

Juice of 1/2 lemon

INSTRUCTIONS:

Melt butter and add remaining ingredients. Brush on chicken as it grills. Enough for 1 large chicken.

Different Barbecue Sauce

1 cup brown sugar

1/2 teaspoon garlic powder

1 teaspoon oregano

2 1/4 teaspoons paprika

1 teaspoon seasoned salt

1 teaspoon chili powder

1/2 teaspoon ground cloves

1 teaspoon black pepper

2 tablespoons whole mustard seed

1 bay leaf

2 tablespoons onion

6 tablespoons wine vinegar

1/4 cup olive oil

1/2 cup water

1 can (8 oz.) tomato sauce

2 tablespoons Worcestershire sauce

INSTRUCTIONS:

Mix dry ingredients together first; add rest of ingredients. Cook in a saucepan on medium heat until mixture is hot, then turn to low and cook for 30 minutes.

Side Dishes

Garbage Bread

INGREDIENTS:

1 loaf garlic bread

1/2 cup butter

3 teaspoons garlic powder

1 small onion, chopped

1/4 green pepper, chopped

1 package pepperoni

2 cups shredded cheese

INSTRUCTIONS:

Place bread on its side and cut in half lengthwise. Melt butter with the garlic powder and butter both inside sections of the bread. Spread the onions and green peppers, pepperoni and cheese on one portion of the bread. Place the other bread portion on top. Wrap in aluminum foil and bake in oven or on the grill until cheese is melted. Let cool a couple of minutes before cutting and serving.

Potatoes on the Grill

INGREDIENTS:

4 medium potatoes

1 onion

4 tablespoons butter

1/3 cup cheddar cheese, shredded

1 tablespoon Worcestershire sauce

1 tablespoon parsley

1 chicken bouillon cube

Salt and pepper to taste

Heavy duty aluminum foil

INSTRUCTIONS:

Peel and thinly slice potatoes. Cut the onion into slices. Dissolve the bouillon cube in 1/3 cup of hot water.

Place the onion and potatoes on a large piece of heavy duty aluminum foil. (about 20" x 20"). Add slices of butter on top of the potatoes. Mix the cheese, Worcestershire sauce and parsley together and add on top of the butter. Sprinkle with salt and pepper. Fold up the sides of the foil to make a bowl and add the hot water with dissolved bouillon cube. Seal the foil into a packet. Grill, covered, over medium heat for 40 minutes or until potatoes are tender.

Yield: Serves 4.

BBQ-Side Garden Salad

INGREDIENTS:

2 tomatoes, seeded and chopped

1 cup frozen whole kernel corn

1 zucchini, diced

1/3 cup green onions, thinly sliced

1 small avocado, chopped

1/3 cup picante sauce

2 tablespoons cilantro, chopped

2 tablespoons vegetable oil

1 tablespoon lemon juice or lime juice

1/4 teaspoon ground cumin

3/4 teaspoon garlic salt

INSTRUCTIONS:

Combine the tomatoes, corn, zucchini, green onions and avocado in a large bowl. In a smaller bowl, combine the picante sauce, oil, cilantro, lemon juice, cumin and garlic salt and stir to mix. Pour the picante sauce mixture over the vegetables and toss gently. Refrigerate, covered, for 3 to 4 hours, stirring occasionally. Serve chilled.

Yield: Serves 4.

Other books by Justin A. Bryant

Available at Amazon.com in Kindle and Paperback formats.